IMAGES
of England

ALDERSHOT

A MILITARY TOWN

MAP OF ALDERSHOT COMMAND.

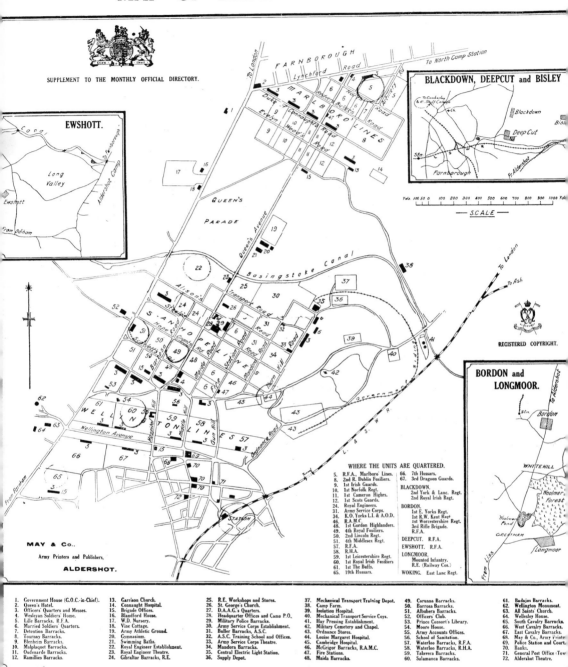

SUPPLEMENT TO THE MONTHLY OFFICIAL DIRECTORY.

EWSHOTT.

BLACKDOWN, DEEPCUT and BISLEY

BORDON and LONGMOOR.

REGISTERED COPYRIGHT.

MAY & Co.,

Army Printers and Publishers,

ALDERSHOT.

WHERE THE UNITS ARE QUARTERED.

No.	Unit	No.	Unit
5.	R.F.A., Marlboro' Lines.	66.	7th Hussars.
8.	2nd R. Dublin Fusiliers.	67.	3rd Dragoon Guards.
9.	1st Irish Guards.		
10.	1st Norfolk Regt.		**BLACKDOWN.**
11.	1st Cameron Highrs.		2nd York & Lanc. Regt.
12.	1st Scots Guards.		2nd Royal Irish Regt.
24.	Royal Engineers.		**BORDON.**
31.	Army Service Corps.		1st E. Yorks Regt.
34.	K.O. Yorks L.I. & A.O.D.		1st R.W. Kent Regt
46.	R.A.M.C.		1st Worcestershire Regt.
48.	1st Gordon Highlanders.		3rd Rifle Brigade.
49.	4th Royal Fusiliers.		R.F.A.
50.	2nd Lincoln Regt.		**DEEPCUT.** R.F.A.
51.	4th Middlesex Regt.		
57.	R.F.A.		**EWSHOTT.** R.F.A.
58.	R.H.A.		**LONGMOOR.**
59.	1st Leicestershire Regt.		Mounted Infantry.
60.	1st Royal Irish Fusiliers		R.E. (Railway Cos.)
61.	1st The Buffs.		
65.	19th Hussars.		**WOKING.** East Lanc Regt.

No.		No.		No.	
1.	Government House (G.O.C.-in-Chief).	25.	R.E. Workshops and Stores.	49.	Corunna Barracks.
2.	Queen's Hotel.	26.	St. George's Church.	50.	Barrosa Barracks.
3.	Officers' Quarters and Messes.	27.	D.A.A.G.'s Quarters.	51.	Albuhera Barracks.
4.	Wesleyan Soldiers' Home.	28.	Headquarter Offices and Camp P.O.	52.	Officers' Club.
5.	Lille Barracks. R.F.A.	29.	Military Police Barracks.	53.	Prince Consort's Library.
6.	Married Soldiers' Quarters.	30.	Army Service Corps Establishment.	54.	Moore House.
7.	Detention Barracks.	31.	Buller Barracks, A.S.C.	55.	Army Accounts Offices.
8.	Tournay Barracks.	32.	A.S.C. Training School and Offices.	56.	School of Sanitation.
9.	Blenheim Barracks.	33.	Army Service Corps Theatre.	57.	Waterloo Barracks, R.F.A.
10.	Malplaquet Barracks.	34.	Mandora Barracks.	58.	Waterloo Barracks, R.H.A.
11.	Oudenarde Barracks.	35.	Central Electric Light Station.	59.	Talavera Barracks.
12.	Ramillies Barracks.	36.	Supply Depot.	60.	Salamanca Barracks.
13.	Garrison Church.	37.	Mechanical Transport Training Depot.	61.	Badajos Barracks.
14.	Connaught Hospital.	38.	Camp Farm.	62.	Wellington Monument.
15.	Brigade Offices.	39.	Isolation Hospital.	63.	All Saints' Church.
16.	Blandford House.	40.	Mechanical Transport Service Coys.	64.	Wellesley House.
17.	W.D. Nursery.	41.	Hay Pressing Establishment.	65.	South Cavalry Barracks.
18.	Vine Cottage.	42.	Military Cemetery and Chapel.	66.	West Cavalry Barracks.
19.	Army Athletic Ground.	43.	Ordnance Stores.	67.	East Cavalry Barracks.
20.	Gymnasium.	44.	Louise Margaret Hospital.	68.	May & Co., Army Printers
21.	Swimming Baths.	45.	Cambridge Hospital.	69.	Police Station and Court.
22.	Royal Engineer Establishment.	46.	McGrigor Barracks, R.A.M.C.	70.	Banks.
23.	Royal Engineer Theatre.	47.	Fire Stations.	71.	General Post Office (Town
24.	Gibraltar Barracks, R.E.	48.	Maida Barracks.	72.	Aldershot Theatre.

Aldershot Command, layout of barracks, 1909/10.

2

IMAGES
of England

ALDERSHOT
A MILITARY TOWN

Compiled by
Ian Maine

TEMPUS

First published 2002
Copyright © Ian Maine, 2002

Tempus Publishing Limited
The Mill, Brimscombe Port,
Stroud, Gloucestershire, GL5 2QG

ISBN 0 7524 2465 3

Typesetting and origination by
Tempus Publishing Limited
Printed in Great Britain by
Midway Colour Print, Wiltshire

Contents

Acknowledgements   6

Introduction   7

1.   Home   9

2.   People   25

3.   Routine   35

4.   Regiments   47

5.   Training and Skills   63

6.   Joining   75

7   National Service   81

8   Leisure and Welfare   87

9   Technology   103

10   Departures   113

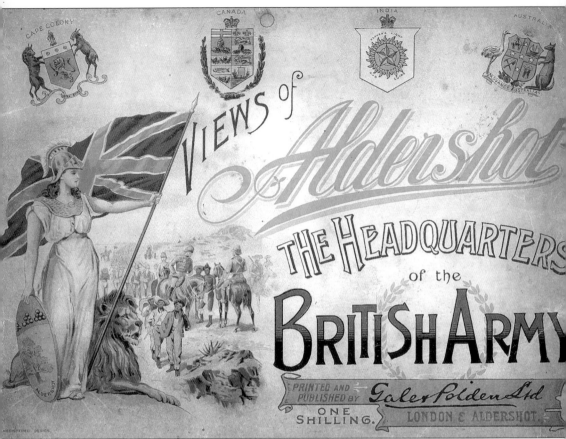

Aldershot – Headquarters of the British Army – lithograph cover, *c.* 1900.

Acknowledgements

This book has been compiled entirely from the collections of the Aldershot Military Museum. It follows therefore, that my thanks are due to the large numbers of people who visit the museum and who leave objects and photographs for the collections. It is only through these acts of generosity that the richness of the museum's collections can be enhanced and made available for others to enjoy.

My special thanks are also due to my colleagues at the museum, Sally Day and Hannah Whitmill, who undertook the unenviable task of finding and retrieving all of the images from the museum's photographic store.

Ian Maine
Curator of the Aldershot Military Museum

Introduction

For several decades, Aldershot has been known as 'The Home of the British Army'. I was delighted to be able to compile this selection of images from the collections of the Aldershot Military Museum, to compliment the earlier selection produced on the civic, rather than military, Aldershot.

The arrival of the Army in Aldershot in 1854 happened just before the process of army reform had really begun, but neatly coincides with the early development of photography, ensuring that all periods of Aldershot's military history are recorded in that medium.

Aldershot quickly changed from the original concept of a temporary camp to a permanent one. By the end of the 1890s, the camp had grown to be the largest British military garrison in the British Empire, at a time when a quarter of the world's population were encompassed within it. Military Aldershot was far more than a collection of barracks, however. It was a complete military town. It had its own water and power supply, meat and bread production, police force, prison and fire brigade. It included training facilities for both regular and auxiliary forces from subjects as diverse as physical training, signalling, ballooning, gas warfare, equitation, and veterinary medicine.

It was from this peak in the 1890s from which Aldershot projected troops onto the world's stage. Troops had travelled from Aldershot from as early as 1857 to India, and departures for the Egyptian and other campaigns all over the globe were also made in the years up to 1899. It was the mobilization for South Africa in that year which tested Aldershot as a military machine. The mobilization itself was a great success, providing troops with foreign service equipment, kitting-out reservists, and training some of the tens of thousands of Imperial Yeomanry who had volunteered to fight. The war itself was less successful, beset with supply problems and the employment of tactics inappropriate for both the terrain in which they were fighting, and the enemy they faced.

After the South African War ended in 1902, a further series of Army reforms were undertaken, producing by 1914 the best army Britain had ever had. The 1st and 2nd Divisions of this Army were based within the Aldershot Command. The survivors of this Army from the First World War were known as the 'Old Contemptibles,' and their reunions were naturally centred on Aldershot until they were discontinued in 1974.

The period after the First World War saw the beginnings of change for the Army in Aldershot: the development of a dedicated signals service housed in Mons Barracks, and the mechanization of the Army – which saw both tank testing around Farnborough as well as the basing of two battalions of the Royal Tanks Corps there until 1939. Significantly too, there was the emergence of new centres for military training at Catterick, Tidworth and Bulford.

The Second World War again saw the departure of another British Expeditionary Force (BEF) for France, and the almost exclusive use of the camp by the Canadian Army. Following the war, the extension of conscription until 1960 was very much in evidence in the large numbers of eighteen year old recruits who were posted to Aldershot at some point in their training. Not least of all, was the basing of Britain's Parachute Brigade at Aldershot from 1947, an association which lasted for over fifty years.

It is important to remember that most of the occupants of the garrison would only stay in Aldershot for a relatively brief period of time. This could range from a few weeks for a National

Serviceman to a few years for a normal tour. In any event, Aldershot would form a brief, though probably memorable interlude within a military career.

Many of the views in this compilation though 'military' are informal – very little of the official photography routinely taken by the Army for its own purposes has been reproduced here. The photographs include work by a number of well known local photographers, not least of which is Gale and Polden, who as well as a printing and publishing business, had a very prolific photographic studio. Images include those commissioned by military units, postcards, and albums compiled by a few people who had the wherewithal to take their own photographs – no other garrison could provide such a diverse selection of images.

Cover for badge poster, showing the Royal Field Artillery, printed by Gale & Polden, *c.* 1910.

One

Home

View of the Infantry Barracks, c. 1860. Constructed between 1856 and 1859, these were part of a series of 'permanent barracks'. The permanent barracks consisted of those for cavalry, artillery and infantry. There were three infantry barracks – East, Central and West which were subsequently re-named Badajos, Talavera and Salamanca.

Construction of gates to the cavalry barracks, Aldershot, 1856. For each of Aldershot's cavalry barracks, there was a gateway similar to this one. Behind the gates would be a guard room, orderly room and small cell block to house soldiers who arrived back at barracks drunk. Two of these gateways survive today, one on the Wellington roundabout, the other on the Farnborough Road.

Building materials at Aldershot, 1856. The programme of barracks building at Aldershot was a huge financial commitment by the War Department. Much of the brick, stone, wood and other materials to erect the buildings was brought to Aldershot via the Basingstoke Canal, as Aldershot did not receive a direct rail link until 1870.

Construction work at Aldershot Cavalry Barracks, 1856. The permanent barracks were all built to very high standards, and incorporated findings of the Army sanitary commission, which had recommended changes to the living accommodation for soldiers. Above is one of three riding schools built to enable cavalry training to be undertaken in the dry. Below is some of the extensive troop stabling to house the significant numbers of horses which would form Aldershot's Cavalry Brigade.

Hut in 'S' Lines, South Camp, *c.* 1890. Soon after the Army had begun to arrive in Aldershot in 1854, two large areas of wooden huts were constructed. Each was designed to accommodate a division of infantry, and were named North and South Camps. Each of the lines of huts was referred to by a letter. Although designed as 'temporary', they all survived into the 1890s, when they were replaced by brick-built barracks.

Warburg Barrack gates, *c.* 1950. These gates formed a very familiar land mark at the top of the High Street in Aldershot, and illustrated the division between town and camp. Originally known as the East Cavalry Barracks, they were renamed Warburg Barracks in 1909, to commemorate the Battle of Warburg in 1760. Demolished in 1964 the site is now occupied by a car park known as the Warburg car park. The site is also occupied by the Princes Hall, a Civic Hall completed in the early 1970s.

Aerial view, Beaumont Barracks, c. 1970. Beaumont Barracks, originally known as the South Cavalry Barracks, was the last of Aldershot's fine Victorian cavalry barracks to be demolished. This aerial view shows the officers' mess at the top of the photograph. Below that is the sergeants' mess, above the riding school. It was in this riding school that Churchill would have undertaken his military riding course on his posting to Aldershot in the 1890s. On either side of these buildings is the troop stabling, shared by troopers and horses alike. Demolished in 1975, the site is now occupied by housing, with the exception of the retaining wall, veterinary stables and the riding school, which were listed and saved from the bull dozer.

Troop stables – Willems Barracks, 1963. Aldershot had three main cavalry barracks, all built between 1856 and 1859, known as the Warburg, Willems and Beaumont Barracks. The mechanization of the Army during the 1930s had made rows of troop stabling like this redundant and difficult to adapt for modern military use. All three barracks were demolished from 1959 onwards, with these particular troop stables being demolished shortly after these pictures were taken.

Barrossa Barracks,
Stanhope Lines, 1897-
1962. Barrossa Barracks
was part of a huge
scheme of barrack
building, which replaced
the old huts. Each of the
major areas was referred
to by a collective term –
in this period it was
either Marlborough,
Stanhope or Wellington
Lines. Each barracks
within a lines would be
appropriately named
after a battle. The two-
storey soldiers'
accommodation is shown
virtually new above,
whilst the demise of the
barracks' fine officers
mess is shown on the
right, when the barracks
had to make way for
Montgomery Lines.

Hospital Hill – from a post card by May's, Aldershot, c. 1870. Known as Union building, this is one of the few buildings in the area from the era before the arrival of the Army. It was in use as a work house. However, by the time this photograph was taken, it had been converted for use as a military hospital. It subsequently became a pay office and now is in use as a facility for military families. The fountain in the fore ground was demolished in the 1930s as part of a scheme of traffic improvements, and the busy road junction of today has none of the charm of this view.

Redan Hill Camp, Government Sidings and Field Stores, 1905. Aldershot was much more than a collection of barracks. It became a complete system for mobilizing troops and equipping them at short notice. The government sidings and stores meant that men, equipment and stores could be drawn together and sent off by rail quickly and effectively.

Number 36 Hut, Pinehurst Barracks, Farnborough, 1918. Pinehurst Barracks was established during the First World War and consisted initially of wooden huts like the one in the picture. These wooden huts were replaced by brick buildings in the 1930s, when the barracks were renamed Elles Barracks. The group of men in this picture are photographed having won the third prize for best kept hut and garden in the barracks.

Talavera Barracks from Aldershot High Street, c. 1950. Princes Gardens – in the fore ground – are where the Royal Engineers established their works area when the Army first came to Aldershot in the 1850s. This area has always marked one of the boundaries between town and camp.

Grant Square, 1893 and Cowie Square, Buller Barracks, *c.* 1950. During the 1890s rebuilding of Aldershot, several squares of married quarters were built. At the time they represented significant improvement compared to the allocations of barrack huts which had previously been made to men on the 'married strength' of a regiment. Most of these squares were demolished during the 1960s rebuilding of Aldershot.

Above: Napier Square married quarters, *c.* 1970. One group of 1890s married quarters in North Camp, Napier Square, stood at the northern end of Queens Avenue. These were not demolished until the late 1980s (*below*), by which time they had become very run down, and provided a poor quality of accommodation to their occupants. After they were demolished, the site was turned into a car park with adjoining garden, pond and water feature.

Royal Pavilion, Aldershot, c. 1950. Military Aldershot once boasted a royal residence. One of the first buildings to be constructed in Aldershot after the arrival of the Army was the Royal Pavilion, originally referred to as the 'Queens Pavilion'. It was in this modest royal palace that members of the Royal Family would stay when visiting the area to review troops or present colours. The lower photograph shows men of the Cameronians (Scottish Rifles) in 1926, passing the front gates to the pavilion saluting King George V. The gates and railings shown in this picture survive today, though the Royal Pavilion itself was demolished in 1963.

Aerial view of Stanhope Lines, c. 1963. At the time this photograph was taken, only the barracks in the lower left had been demolished to make way for Montgomery Lines. Maida Barracks on the lower right still stands, as does Gibraltar Barracks, centre left. All of these areas would fall to the bull dozer before the close of the decade.

Aerial view, Montgomery Lines, c. 1965. Taken a couple of years after the previous photograph, the newly completed Montgomery Lines area is visible at the top of the image. Gibraltar Barracks is now subject to the attention of the demolition firms. Also visible in the centre right is a line of pre-cast concrete sections which would form the basis of the buildings of Browning Barracks which would be built on this site.

Demolition of Salamanca Barracks, 1960. Following the abolition of National Service in 1960, Aldershot no longer required the same quantity of living accommodation for single soldiers. Salamanca Barracks – completed in 1859 – was one of the first of Aldershot's Victorian barrack blocks to be demolished to make way for the new military town of the 1960s.

Demolition of Blenheim Barracks, North Camp, 1965. Built as infantry barracks in the 1890s, they served as a home for soldiers prior to departure for South Africa in 1899, France in 1914 or 1939, and latterly for conscripted National Servicemen. The ending of National Service saw them become redundant and before long, they were demolished and replaced by married quarters – in this case, Blenheim Park married quarters.

Married Quarters, Talavera Park, c. 1965. These married quarters replaced Talavera Infantry Barracks as part of the Army's desire to improve and increase married quarter provision. Although completed in 1965, the design and construction of these quarters was so poor that they were demolished in 1989 and replaced by semi detached housing of far superior design and quality.

Construction of Montgomery Lines, 1964. One of the cornerstones of the redevelopment for the military town in the 1960s was a barracks complex to house Aldershot's Parachute Brigade. Most of the elements of this would be quartered in Montgomery Lines. Four separate barrack areas were constructed along with associated workshops and stores.

Queen Alexandra Royal Army Nursing Corps Training Centre, 1966. Taken just before its completion, this training centre was always referred to as the Royal Pavilion – the single storey Royal Palace built in 1856 which it replaced. The building technique used to construct Aldershot's new barracks in the 1960s, including this one, was an industrialized form of construction, which utilized pre-cast concrete sections, bolted together and topped with flat roofs. When the training of the Army Medical Services was reorganized, the Queen Alexandra Royal Army Nursing Corps no longer required the building. The training centre was eventually demolished in 1998, when the site was sold off for redevelopment as offices.

Two

People

ROYAL REVIEW
Laffans Plain,
ALDERSHOT.
1st July, 1897.
ADMIT BEARER
TO
GRAND STAND.
SECTION. F.   SEAT Nº 373

CALE & POLDEN Lᵗᵈ LONDON & ALDERSHOT

Ticket for Queen Victoria's Diamond Jubilee Review, 1 July 1897. Queen Victoria visited Aldershot almost every year from 1854 until 1898. Royal reviews became a regular part of camp life. This ticket was for one of the last reviews she saw, with no less than 27,000 troops on parade.

Lt-Gen. Sir William T. Knollys KCB, First General Officer Commanding 'The Camp at Aldershott', May 1855-June 1860. Commissioned into 3rd (later Scots) Guards when just sixteen, he saw action in the Peninsular War and crossed into France seeing fighting at Bayonne, and the crossing of the Adour river. He returned home in 1814 and later commanded his regiment. It was during this period that he instructed the Prince Consort in military affairs, which eventually led to his appointment at Aldershot. A fine administrator, he was instrumental in organizing the commissariat and medical services. In his early days at Aldershot, he personally had to instruct the troops in such elementary matters as pitching tents!. Promoted to General in 1866, he became Comptroller to the Prince of Wales and later Gentleman Usher of the Black Rod at Westminster, where he died in June 1883 at the age of eighty-five. In Aldershot he is remembered in Knollys road at the top of hospital hill.

Staff of Aldershot District, c. 1891. General Sir Evelyn Wood VC was the General Officer Commanding (GOC) from 1889-1893. He is shown here (middle row, fourth from left) with his staff outside of the modest group of huts, which provided his headquarters building until they were replaced in 1894 by the brick building which still stands today.

The body of Field Marshal Sir Evelyn Wood VC lying in state, Royal Garrison church Aldershot, December 1919. On his death, Evelyn Wood's body was taken to the Royal Garrison Church. His body is guarded by a detachment of Warrant officers and NCOs from the 17th Lancers, one of the regiments with which he had served in a long and distinguished career.

HRH Duke of Connaught, 1896. The Duke of Connaught was the third son of Queen Victoria. He commanded Aldershot District from October 1893 to October 1898. Born on 1 May 1850, he held commissions in various regiments including the Royal Engineers, Royal Artillery, Rifle Brigade and 7th Hussars. He held several staff appointments in Aldershot and commanded a brigade from September 1880-1883 including a Brigade of Guards during the short Egyptian campaign of August-November 1882. During his time as General Officer Comanding at Aldershot, he oversaw the bulk of the re-building of the camp and a series of manoeuvres of a size and complexity never seen before. He lived in Bagshot Park, Surrey and died in January 1942, aged ninety-one.

Quarter Master Sergeant Branson, 1890. Branson, pictured to the rear right of the group here, had been in the Rifle Brigade but was posted to Aldershot where he worked at Divisional Headquarters as a clerk. He retired to the town and became heavily involved with the work of the Church of England Soldiers Institute in Victoria Road, where he eventually became manager.

Sergeant Major William Moore, Royal Flying Corps, 1912. Along with most of the Royal Flying Corps, William Moore began his military career in the Royal Engineers, with whom he enlisted in 1889. He became a balloonist in the Royal Engineers at Aldershot and served in the South African War (1899-1902). (Photograph taken by John Russell, Photographer, South Farnborough.)

HM King George V accompanied by Lt-Gen. Sir Douglas Haig at Aldershot, May 1914. Taken a few months before the First World War, the upper view shows troops being inspected on Queens Parade, whilst the lower view shows the men on part of Aldershot's training grounds. The King always took a keen interest in the Army and frequently came down to observe military manoeuvres on horse back.

Field Marshal Sir William Robertson. William Robertson enjoys the rare distinction of being one of the very few people to rise from private to Field Marshal. Robertson joined the army as a private in the 16th Lancers. As a cavalry man, he was posted with the regiment to Willems Barracks in 1879. Following promotion through the ranks and a commission in 1890, he returned again to Aldershot in 1908 on the command staff as a Brigadier-General. He subsequently went on to become Chief of the Imperial General Staff (CIGS) during the First World War. He died in 1933, and renewed his connection with the area being buried in nearby Brookwood Military Cemetery.

Lt-Gen. Sir Horace Smith-Dorrien KCB DSO, General Officer Commanding at Aldershot, 1907 to 1912. Born 26 May 1858, Smith-Dorrien was commissioned in February 1876, aged eighteen. By 1900, he was serving in South Africa as a Major General, before going to India from 1901 to 1907. In December 1907, he was GOC at Aldershot and promoted to the rank of General in 1912. During the First World War, Smith Dorrien was returned to England by the Chief of the Imperial General Staff, William Robertson, who dropped his 'H's with the words ''Orace, you're for 'ome!'. Following the war, Smith-Dorrien was Governor and Commander-in-Chief of Gibraltar. He died in 1930, aged eighty-eight.

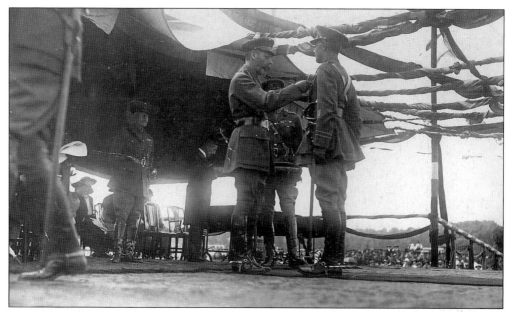

King George V presenting the Victoria Cross to Capt. A.M. Toye of the Middlesex Regiment, Queens Parade, Aldershot, June 1918. Alfred Maurice Toye was born in the married quarters in Stanhope Lines in 1897. He had won his VC in France in March 1918; he is one of only two people from Aldershot to win the Victoria Cross.

King George VI inspecting Canadian Troops, 1940. Regular royal visits continued in Aldershot until the Second World War. This pattern was disrupted on the outbreak of war. Despite this, when Aldershot became a huge training centre for thousands of Canadian Troops, several royal visits were arranged to help cement relations with the Dominion of Canada. Here the King inspects the Royal Canadian Regiment at Guillemont Barracks, Cove.

Lady Patricia Ramsay (formerly Princess Patricia of Connaught), with Lt-Col. Colquhoun (right) and Maj. J.N. Edgar, Morval Barracks, Cove 1940. Lady Ramsay is pictured here visiting the Princess Patricia's Canadian Light Infantry (PPCLI), who were stationed at Cove at the time. These barracks were one of a number of camps built during the 1930s. They incorporated many new facilities, including dining halls and even a cinema. The soldiers huts followed a layout, whereby individual huts were linked with covered corridors, and the hutting arrangements quickly became known as 'spiders'.

Nursing Staff, 8th Canadian General Hospital, Aldershot, 1943. Following the departure of all of Aldershot's regular soldiers in September 1939 as part of the British Expeditionary Force (BEF), the camp was used as a base by the Canadian Army overseas. The Canadian Forces included female service personnel who worked in Aldershot's military hospitals.

Three
Routine

Time Gun, Gun Hill, *c.* 1910. From 1856 until 1914, a time gun was sounded twice daily. Added to the bugle calls for all parts of the daily routine there were few excuses, even for soldiers without a watch, not to know what you were supposed to be doing at any point in the working day.

Special Programme

OF THE VISIT OF

THEIR MAJESTIES

The King and Queen

.. TO ..

ALDERSHOT,

On June 14th, 1902.

ALSO OF THE

GRAND TORCHLIGHT TATTOO

AND THE ORGANISATION OF TROOPS TAKING PART

IN THE

ROYAL REVIEW

To be held Monday, June 16th,

ON LAFFAN'S PLAIN.

Printed and Sold by Gale & Polden, Ltd., Wellington Works, Aldershot.

Programme for a Grand Searchlight Tattoo and Royal Review, Aldershot, 1902. The searchlight tattoo was the pre cursor to Aldershot's world famous tattoos of the 1920s and '30s. Royal reviews continued to be held regularly until the late 1930s but they weren't revived after the Second World War.

Royal Review on Laffan's Plain, Aldershot, 10 June 1924. Laffan's Plain was levelled in the 1860s to provide a camping ground and parade area. It fulfilled these functions for many years, until it was brought into use as an airfield prior to the First World War. Today the area is used for business aviation.

Guard, Oudenarde Barracks, 1904. Although not always behind walls or barbed wire, each of the barracks within Aldershot had to provide its own guard. At certain times of the day, or for specific occasions, a regiment would have to 'turn out the guard'. Here, the Irish Guards turn out at the guard room of Oudenarde Barracks. These barracks were constructed during the 1890s and were mostly demolished in 1965, with the exception of two barrack blocks which now house the Aldershot Military Museum.

Kitchen, Royal Army Medical Corps Depot, *c.* 1910. By the Edwardian period, the cuisine of the Army had gradually improved. This was a direct result of better trained cooks, more carefully selected rations and vastly superior equipment. Some of this equipment is in evidence in this image by local photographer J.H. West.

Drawing rations, 10th Hussars, *c.* 1900. Every morning the bread and meat allocated to each group of men was drawn from the quartermaster. The bread was then distributed, and the meat taken to the cook house. A frequent cause of complaint was that the $\frac{3}{4}$lb meat allocated to each man per day included fat, bone and gristle, and that frequently the married soldiers and non-commissioned officers would receive the best cuts of the meat available.

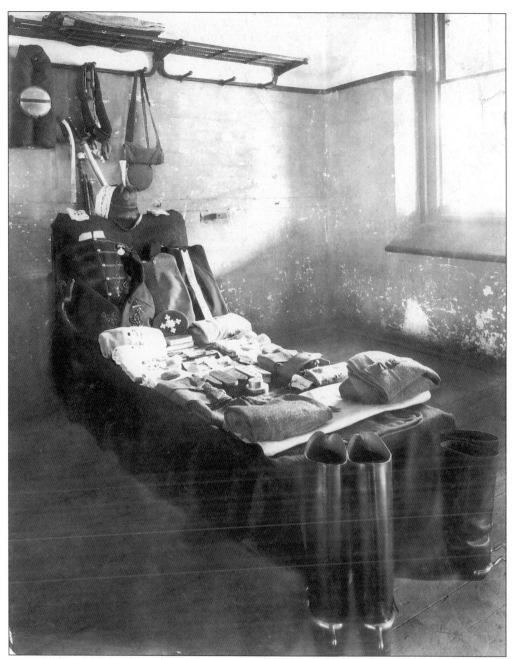

Kit lay out, 13th Hussars, 1904. This regiment was quartered in the East (later Warburg) Cavalry Barracks when this was taken by local printers and publishers Gale and Polden. An important element of any Victorian or Edwardian soldiers routine was the periodic inspection of everything issued to him by the government. Any deficiencies were soon spotted as each soldier had to lay his kit out in exactly the same way – the reason photos such as this were taken. To prevent soldiers stealing or swapping items of kit, everything was marked with the man's regimental number – clearly seen on several of the items in this picture.

21st (Empress of India's) Lancers watering horses in barracks, c. 1903. The life of a cavalry man revolved around the care of his horse and everything connected with it, whether he was in barracks or on maneouvres. Here horses are given water – clearly visible in the background is the austere troop stabling which provided stalls for horses below, and barrack rooms for men above. The compensation of this arrangement was the heat from the horses below, which provided warmth to the otherwise cold rooms above.

Drawing forage for horses, 10th Hussars, c. 1900. Another element of daily routine for the cavalry soldier was drawing the regulation amount of forage for each troop of horses in large bundles, which was then distributed amongst them. The quartermaster's staff are very much in evidence (right) to ensure the prescribed quantities were adhered to by the stablemen.

Non-Commissioned Officers Mess, Royal Engineers, Aldershot, c. 1910. An important element of routine for the non-commissioned and officers in any regiment was mess life. For these men the mess provided comforts not available to the other ranks within the rest of the unit. However for officers in particular mess bills could add up considerably. In some regiments mess bills exceeded an army officer's salary, necessitating another means of income to meet any shortfall.

Saddlers, 3rd Reserve Cavalry Regiment, Aldershot, 1917. Repair and up keep of a cavalry regiment's saddlery and tack was a continual process. Here a group of saddlers pause for the camera. The man seated front right is holding a rifle bucket – designed for keeping a rifle on the saddle. The 3rd Reserve Cavalry Regiment was one of a number of reserve cavalry regiments established to provide drafts to the regular and Yeomanry Cavalry regiments serving overseas during the First World War. Seated front centre is Saddler Sergeant J. Kinally.

Breakfast for man and horse and preparing tea, Manoeuvres in Berkshire, 1893. Every year troops from Aldershot would travel to one of a number of places such as the New Forest or Salisbury Plain where larger scale manoeuvres could take place. These were huge logistical operations. They tested not only the ability of an Army based on horse and foot to cover distances, but also the capacity of the its support arms to supply the needs of horses and men.

Preparing dinner and an evening shave, Aldershot Manoeuvres, 1893. In both images the water cart can be seen. Drinking water was normally taken on manoeuvres as the quality of the supply to be found on a camping site could not always be guaranteed. Military routines of shaving every day were still strictly adhered to despite the primitive facilities.

Tailors shop, Buller Barracks, *c.* 1910. Albert Hodges ran a tailors shop supplying the continuous needs of a variety of regiments who were always expected to be well turned out. He is pictured in a suit on the right at the far end of the table.

The 'Glass House', Aldershot, 1908. For soldiers in Aldershot who made more serious breeches of military discipline, the Detention Centre, situated in North Camp, was where they would spend a period of time ranging from a few days to several months. The detention centre was soon christened the glass house owing to its glazed sky lights.

The Governor's office, Aldershot Military Detention Centre, 1908. Admissions to the galls house were made everyday at 2 p.m., and people would queue outside the centre's austere walls. For soldiers confined there, tasks would range from sewing military feed bags, various sorts of physical exercise or mat making, shown here.

Kit layout belonging to Jack Matthews, Royal Army Service Corps, in Buller Barracks., 1954. Jack Matthews joined the Army at fifteen as a boy farrier. The Army Sevice Corps, (later Royal) has a long association with Aldershot. At this time, the Royal Army Service Corps still maintained a small number of horses in Aldershot which were used to pull General Service Wagons to make local deliveries. The horse transport squadron was maintained until 1970 when it was finally disbanded.

Four
Regiments

Private, Royal Scots Greys, Infirmary Stables, Aldershot, c. 1893. The Scots Greys were the only cavalry regiment to mount all of their soldiers on grey horses. This very rare photograph is evidence of Aldershot's provision of infirmary stables in the 1860s, as part of a move towards better veterinary care for its horses.

Cooks, 1st Battalion Manchester Regiment, 1897. An 'instructional kitchen' was established in Aldershot as early as 1856 for the training of cooks (the Army Catering Corps was not established until 1940). This was the Army's first attempt to train cooks, before that time the choice of cooks was based on the man's fitness for service, rather than for his culinary skills. This regiment was quartered in Barrosa Barracks in 1897.

Peeling potatoes, No. 5 Squadron Royal Flying Corps, Aldershot, 1913. On its formation in 1912 in Aldershot from the Air Battalion Royal Engineers, the Royal Flying Corps continued as an Army unit until 1918 when the Royal Air Force was created from it.

Grenadier Guards, Blenheim Barracks, North Camp, 1904. The Grenadiers are shown here wearing their white drill jackets – a form of undress uniform worn at this time by only a few regiments. The Brodrick cap is also worn, which was replaced the following year by a peaked forage cap.

2nd Battalion East Yorkshire Regiment, North Camp, 1927. The guard of the battalion is pictured here turned out at Malplaquet Barracks. Guards would operate a twenty-four hour routine and would be changed daily. The guard also formed the fire piquet, the equipment for which is in evidence underneath the verandah.

A Highlander, Blenheim Barracks, *c.* 1920. A typical soldier at the end of the First World War, complete with kilt apron and gas mask. The steel helmet had been introduced in 1916 to reduce the number of casualties from shrapnel wounds to the head. The site is now occupied by Wavell Secondary School, although in the back ground can be seen the Queens Hotel, which still stands today.

3rd Carabiniers, Beaumont Barracks, 1933. From 1859 until 1938 Aldershot's Cavalry brigade housed at one time or another every British cavalry regiment, with the exception of the Household Cavalry. They provided a colourful spectacle to the populations of both the military and civilian towns. The 3rd Carabiners shown here were an amalgamation of the 3rd Dragoon Guards and The Carabiniers (6th Dragoon Guards). The amalgamation occurred in 1922 when cuts in the size of the Army saw the reduction of many horsed cavalry regiments.

Drum Horse 'Prince', 2nd Dragoon Guards (Queens Bays), 1936. Taken to commemorate the mechanization of the Regiment whilst they were quartered at Willems Barracks, Aldershot. Drum horses were controlled purely by using the legs, which were attached to reins. Trumpet Major Rutherford is shown seated.

2nd Battalion The Royal Fusiliers, Aldershot Command Searchlight Tattoo, 1926. On the declaration of war in 1914, full dress for the British Army was abolished. For elements of the Aldershot Tattoo it was periodically issued on a temporary basis. For many of the participants in any tattoo, historical costume was improvised and worn. In this case the battalion pictured has adopted viking dress. Whether this was popular with the participants is very much a matter of conjecture, though no doubt it would have been popular with some.

2nd Battalion The Buffs, Aldershot Command Searchlight Tattoo, 1927. Each Aldershot Tattoo had a different historical theme. The 1927 Tattoo featured a recreation of the Battle of Blenheim, complete with a recreated village, French forces and Marlborough's army, part of which is shown here, played by one of Aldershot's resident units.

1st Cavalry Brigade, filming in the Long Valley, Aldershot, 1929. Aldershot's Cavalry men were used for a re-enactment of the Charge of the Light Brigade, which was filmed for the Gainsborough production of *Balaclava*. The site was chosen because of its resemblance to the valley of the Alma where the original charge took place. The charge was directed by Capt. Oakes-Jones MBE FSA, the producer of the Aldershot Tattoos, who acted as the official military adviser to Gainsborough Films. Dummy men and horses were carried among the charging ranks so that when dummy 'Russian shells' dropped among the galloping horses the dummies could be dropped. Russian Dummies were propped against the guns and marked with labels so they could be pierced by Lances or cut down by the swords of the charging cavalry. Trick riders fell from their horses and 'shell bursts' were detonated by electricity and fired by 'dead' men lying on the battlefield.

Military Mounted Police being inspected at Aldershot, 1908. At this time, the military police were divided into two branches – the Military Foot Police and the Military Mounted Police. A new military police headquarters had been completed in Aldershot in 1896.

Royal Artillery Mounted Band, Aldershot Tattoo, Rushmoor Arena, 1939. Mounted Bands were an integral part of the pageantry of the Aldershot Tattoo. The 1939 Tattoo was the last one ever held. The band pictured here was also never to reappear, as the Royal Artillery did not revert to a fully mounted band following the Second World War.

Men of the Toronto Scottish practise Anti-Aircraft drills with Bren Guns, 1940. The Toronto Scottish were one of the Canadian regiments stationed in Aldershot during the early part of the Second World War. The men in this photograph are still wearing the 1908 Pattern Web Equipment, which was obsolete by the time this photograph was taken.

Canadian Infantry, Marlborough Lines, c. 1942. Aldershot became home to tens of thousands of Canadian troops during the Second World War. It was from Aldershot that many of them headed for operations at Dieppe, Sicily and North West Europe.

4th Battalion Royal Canadian Engineers, Farnborough, *c.* 1942. Five Canadian divisions undertook some element of their training in or around Aldershot during 1939-45. Here men at Southwood Camp are inspected by the Camp Commandant and are shown marching past. Southwood Camp was last used by the Royal Engineers who vacated the barracks in 1979. The barracks were demolished and replaced by a housing estate of the same name.

Band of the Royal Canadian Ordnance Corps, Aldershot, 1945. The band is pictured here outside of Warburg Cavalry Barracks, having just received the Freedom of the Borough of Aldershot. The freedom was conferred on the whole Canadian Army, reflecting the close bonds which grew between the Canadians and the town during the Second World War.

Aldershot Area Group Auxiliary Territorial Service (ATS), Waterloo Barracks, 1940. The Second World War was the first time that Aldershot had seen significant numbers of female service personnel. The servicewomen were either members of the ATS shown here, but there were also members of the Canadian Women's Army Corps (CWAC) resident in the camp, as well as large numbers of military nurses.

2nd Battalion Northamptonshire Regiment, Oudenarde Barracks, 1939. This battalion is assembled in battle order. Oudenarde Barracks was completed in the 1890s to house a battalion of infantry. By 1939 some improvements had been made to the barracks including

separate dining facilities and a dental centre. To the rear is the officers mess, whilst on either side is the more modest other ranks accommodation. Each of these blocks would accommodate thirty-eight men.

New Zealand Artillery being inspected by Anthony Eden, Aldershot, 1940. Although Aldershot has been home to virtually every regular regiment of the British Army, it has also seen substantial numbers of foreign or Commonwealth troops in its barracks. These have stayed either as major units as shown above, or smaller numbers of troops or individuals like the Dutch Royal Army Service Corps course pictured below at Mandora Barracks in 1946.

Royal Military Police mounted section, High Street, Aldershot, c. 1950. From its origins in the Military Mounted Police of the 1880s, the Royal Military Police have been a constant presence within Aldershot Military Town. Patrols periodically ventured into the town, as shown here. The last mounted detachment survived at Aldershot until 1995, when its friendly and familiar presence was disbanded, with its horses finally replaced by motorcycles.

The Irish Guards, marching down Queens Avenue, North Camp, c. 1950. Guards Regiments had been regular occupants at Aldershot for many years, though after the Second World War this pattern was broken as Aldershot trained large numbers of National Service conscripts. In the background the recreation rooms of Oudenarde Barracks can be seen, with the North Camp Military Fire Station just beyond. Both of these establishments were demolished in the 1960s.

Viscount Montgomery of Alamein, inspecting Army Physical Training Corps, 1960. The Army Physical training Corps received the Freedom of the Borough of Aldershot in 1960 and are shown here being inspected by Montgomery, along with the Mayor of Aldershot. Montgomery also gave his name to the Parachute Brigade depot, Headquarters and Barracks which were collectively known as 'Montgomery Lines' following their official opening by him in 1965.

Five
Training and Skills

Teaching recruits to shoot, Army Service Corps, 1904. From the introduction of rifled muskets in the 1850s accurate shooting became increasingly important. To enable an instructor to check that his recruit was aiming correctly, tripods like these with a sand bag meant that a recruit's aim could be checked once he had aimed the rifle onto its target. The men here are aiming the Martini-Enfield Carbine and wear the Brodrick cap, one of the shortest lived and least popular items of headdress ever authorized for the Army.

School for officers of Auxiliary Forces, 'M' Lines, South Camp, 1889. Aldershot has been home to a large number of different training establishments over the years. This establishment was based in part of the wooden hutted camp and trained the predecessors to what eventually became the Territorial Army. The officers are wearing various forms of undress uniform, which would have been normal every day wear.

Mounted Infantry Orderly room tent, Aldershot Manoeuvres, 1890. During the 1880s the British Army introduced Mounted Infantry, which could be deployed like infantry, with greater speed, but not as an alternative to cavalry. The mounted infantry training establishment was in North Camp. Aside from the detail in the tent, this illustrates very effectively the way horses in the field were tethered using heel ropes attached to pegs driven into the ground. This was not entirely fool proof however as stampedes amongst horse lines were not unknown.

A linesman asleep, Army Service Corps, on manoeuvres, 1893. Keeping a large force of troops on the move properly supplied was a huge task. In the 1890s significant progress had been made in the logistical support of army formations on the move. Notwithstanding that, the effort on the part of the Army's logistics organizations to keep the military machine properly supplied, involved long hours of exhausting and hard work.

Soldiers asleep at the side of a road, Aldershot Manoeuvres, 1904. For soldiers on foot, not only were long distances covered, but very early starts for marching were often made to enable as much distance to be covered before the hottest part of the day. Regular stops were made. However, even the briefest rest would provide some men with an opportunity to catch up on lost sleep.

A camp near a river, Aldershot Manoeuvres, 1905. When camps were established near rivers troops could wash and bathe their feet. Also shown here are water pumps which would pump water to wood and canvas troughs erected nearby for the horses.

Royal Engineers constructing a bridge over Basingstoke Canal, 1904. Bridging was an important element of the Corps of Royal Engineer's responsibilities. Their barracks in Aldershot were adjacent to the Basingstoke Canal which provided a useful place to hone this particular skill. The spire of one of Aldershot's military churches can be seen in the background.

2nd Volunteer Battalion Queens Regiment, loading baggage before leaving Cove Plateau, August 1903. Although a home for thousands of regular soldiers, Aldershot also witnessed camps of thousands of part-time volunteer soldiers (which subsequently became the Territorial Army). The good rail links meant that many volunteer corps from London would travel to Aldershot and camp for a two week period in the annual manoeuvres season which ran from June to August each year.

A volunteer camp at Aldershot, c. 1900. Aldershot provided a very convenient place for many of London's Volunteer regiments to have their annual training camp. Here the 4th Volunteer Battalion Middlesex Regiment and 2nd London Rifles are pictured outside of the twelve-man tents which would form their accommodation for the duration of their short stay at Aldershot.

Teaching horses to swim at Aldershot, *c.* 1905. It was not only the training of men in Aldershot which was important. The training of horses to overcome all sorts of obstacles was critically important to an army which still relied on the horse for its mobility. To this end a horse swimming pond was constructed on part of Aldershot's training area and used to teach horses how to cross water.

5th (Royal Irish) Lancers, riding exercise near Wellington Statue, *c.* 1904. All of the British Army's Lancer Regiments have been quartered in Aldershot's Cavalry Barracks at one time or another. This regiment is riding back from morning exercise, with the familiar landmark in the back ground. They still wear the Victorian 'Pill box' cap, despite the adoption of the khaki service dress, with which they wear with a bandolier for rifle ammunition.

A cavalry charge, Long Valley, *c.* 1904. Few sights of Edwardian military training would be as impressive as a full scale cavalry charge. One of the most difficult elements of a charge was to keep all the troops and squadrons in line, though this regiment has achieved it. Unfortunately the name of the regiment conducting this charge is unrecorded.

Bayonet Competition, Aldershot, 1904. A non-commissioned officer from the Army Physical Training Staff supervises the competition photographed by Gale and Polden, Aldershot. The rifles were fitted with retractable plungers in place of bayonets.

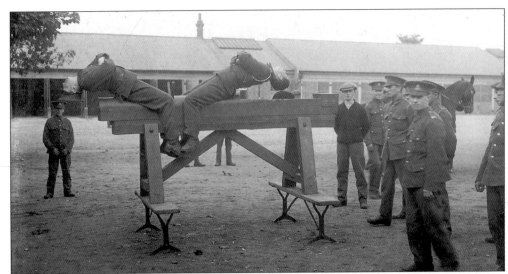

Royal Field Artillery Reserve Regiment, balancing practice, 1917. During the First World War huge numbers of troops were trained at Aldershot, many as part of the 'Kitchener Army', or more correctly 'New Army' divisions. Some troops arrived for training in mounted duties and were posted to reserve cavalry regiments. These units existed to provide drafts of men to the regular cavalry and yeomanry regiments. These men are undertaking balancing practise, which was essential for a mounted man to become proficient at riding (and staying on) a horse.

Vaulting class, Royal Field Artillery, Aldershot, c. 1910. The logical extension of becoming both physically fit and an accomplished horseman, was to undertake feats of precision horsemanship and balance, as demonstrated here. These classes not only built up individual skills, but also working as a team, especially important in horse drawn artillery units.

Soldiers dug in shallow trenches, 1904. Constructing entrenchments like these was an established part of infantry training long before the First World War. The men have discarded their service dress caps which are fitted with coloured bands, which would distinguish them as either enemy or friendly forces.

Bayonet exercise by a Highland Brigade of the 3rd Canadian Division, 20 August 1941. Despite modern technological developments, bayonet fighting was still an important part of basic military training during the Second World War. Here bayonet fighting techniques are practised, though the instructor has ordered that scabbards be kept on the bayonets to prevent injury.

A Royal Engineer, 1939. As well as building field works, bridges and roads the Royal Engineers were also responsible for demolition work. Here, a Royal Engineer is about to blow a large crater in a road during training at Aldershot, just prior to the Second World War.

Training with 3.7-inch Heavy Anti-Aircraft Gun, Beaumont Barracks, 1950. The 3.7 was Britain's main anti-aircraft gun employed during the Second World War. After the war, a Territorial Army unit was established in Aldershot which was equipped with the guns. The riding school at Beaumont Barracks was converted into a large drill shed in which the drill required to bring a gun into action could be practised in the evenings and in poor weather. For actual live gunnery practise, the regiment had to go to Bude, Cornwall where towed targets could be shot at.

· BLOODY ·
BAYONETS

THE COMPLETE GUIDE
TO BAYONET FIGHTING

2nd EDITION

By
Squadron Leader R. A. Lidstone
R.A.F.V.R.

GALE & POLDEN LTD.

Training manual, by Gale and Polden, published in Aldershot, 1940. Gale and Polden published an extensive collection of training manuals which complemented the official War Office publications. They covered a diverse range of subjects from tactics, to gas warfare, shooting and the use of the bayonet (shown here).

Six

Joining

Pay Parade, photographed by Gale and Polden, Aldershot, c. 1902. For many men joining the Army in Victorian and Edwardian Britain, it wasn't only the prospect of regular pay which attracted them to it. For many it provided stability, a sense of purpose and comradeship. For others it was the only alternative to poverty and destitution, or a life of crime.

Poster, 667th Heavy Anti-Aircraft Regiment, Royal Artillery, c. 1950. Aldershot raised a number of Territorial Army units following the Second World War. This Royal Artillery unit was fairly short lived. It was raised in 1947, but disbanded in 1956 when its guns were made obsolete by the advent of rocket technology.

Squads at Drill, Wellington lines, 1904. Soldiers joining infantry regiments were normally trained at a regimental depot before being posted to their regiment. Training then, as today, was a continuous activity – soldiers are seen here undertaking various forms of exercise – physical training, arms drill and aiming practise.

2nd Battalion Worcestershire Regiment arriving at Aldershot in 1913. Joining the Army at any time will almost always involve travel abroad and long periods of separation. Here men arrive back in Britain after seventeen years service overseas – much of it in India, as indicated by the tropical helmets the men are wearing.

Men of the 15th (Scottish) Division, Stanhope Lines, Aldershot, 1914. When Kitchener issued a call for 100,000 volunteers at the outbreak of the First World War, men could not join quickly enough. Soon Aldershot was full of tens of thousands of 'Kitchener men'. The War Office could not keep up with the supply of uniform, equipment or rifles – evidenced here by the men parading in shirt sleeves, with the exception of some of the NCOs.

Men of the 14th (Light) Division, being inspected by King George V, Laffans Plain, 1914. The 'New Army' divisions were normally inspected by a senior military officer, or the King before departing for the front. In the early days the men would still parade before the King in civilian clothes.

Men of the Canadian Army being played in at Government Sidings, Aldershot, 1940. The field stores at Aldershot included a railway siding which could be used for loading and unloading stores and men. On the outbreak of the Second World War, Canada immediately came to Britain's aid, and raised several divisions during the course of the conflict. Here the Royal Artillery band give the Canadians a traditional welcome.

Royal Military College Officer Cadet Training Unit (OCTU), October 1944. Passing out parade of Canadian Officer Cadets, Mons Barracks. Pictured in the front row of the OCTU is RSM R. Brittain, Coldstream Guards who continued at Mons until the late 1950s, and who established a reputation long remembered by many people. It was said his voice on the drill square at Mons could be heard several miles away on a still day!

Guard room, the Parachute Regiment, Maida Barracks, c. 1960. Following the Barracks Act of 1890, Maida Barracks was built along with several other barracks in South Camp, which became known as Stanhope Lines. Until the Second World War, Maida Barracks was occupied by a variety of infantry regiments. Following the war the Parachute Regiment used the barracks as their depot where recruit training would take place. This continued until 1965 when they moved to the newly built Montgomery Lines. Maida Barracks was demolished in 1970 with the exception of its fine gymnasium, still in use today. The Guardroom also went though the tree, planted by General Gordon of Khartoum fame, which survives today.

Seven

National Service

Royal Army Service Corps recruits, North Camp, 1949. These three recruits were some of tens of thousands of National Servicemen who were trained at Aldershot. The Army received far more National Servicemen than both the Royal Navy and Royal Air Force combined.

Jack Skelton Wallace, Evelyn Wood's Road, Ramillies Barracks, 1953. Like so many of his generation, having been conscripted for National Service, Jack Skelton Wallace spent several weeks at Aldershot adjusting to life in the Army. He enlisted into the Army Catering Corps, which trained a large number of its recruits at Aldershot. National Service was introduced in 1948 for every eighteen year old male, and lasted until 1960. Conscription has only been employed twice in Britain, both occasions during the twentieth century.

2nd Training Battalion Royal Army Service Corps, c. 1950. These men are pictured on parade outside of one of the old infantry barracks in Wellington Lines. Aldershot was an important training centre for the Royal Army Service Corps, with most of its intake of young men being trained as drivers or clerks.

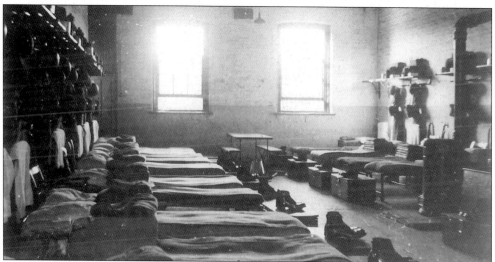

Interior of barrack room, Talavera Barracks, 1949. Talavera Barracks was originally built between 1856 and 1859. After use by Canadian units during the Second World War, it was used for National Servicemen until it was demolished in 1960. This is a typical scene of National Service Army ritual with all of the soldiers' clothing and equipment laid out for inspection. Often soldiers would sleep on the floor the night before an inspection to prevent their perfectly made beds from being spoiled.

Royal Army Service Corps, cleaning kit outside barrack room, Oudenarde Barracks, Aldershot, 1949. This would have been a very familiar sight in Aldershot in the immediate post war years up until the early 1960s. Here webbing equipment is cleaned. The men are wearing 'denims', a washable uniform worn when cleaning, in place of the normal wool serge.

King George V meeting RSM R. Brittain at Mons Barracks, c. 1950. Mons Officer Cadet Training Unit was Aldershot's most famous training unit during the National Service era. During its existence, over 50,000 officers passed out from it. Its most famous Sergeant Major was RSM Brittain, pictured here. Such was his notoriety that he enjoyed a career in advertising and voice-over work after his Army service.

Guard at Mons Barracks, c. 1950. The Guard room was a pivotal part of a military unit's barracks. Here soldiers would be signed in and out of the barracks. Their appearance was always checked before their departure from barracks – hence the mirror visible behind the soldier on the right. Similarly, soldiers returning to barracks late, or drunk could be placed in the cells for the night, before being charged and disciplined for the offence the following day.

Inspection of Guard of Honour, Mons Officer Cadet School, 26 July 1963. During her visit to the town, HM Queen Elizabeth II visited Mons Officer Cadet School. At that time Mons trained many officers from other Commonwealth countries. Mons eventually closed down in 1971, its role being absorbed within the Royal Military Academy at Sandhurst.

Parade, Grosvenor Road, Aldershot, 1954. This parade was staged to celebrate the centenary of the Army's presence in Aldershot. Here, some of the 3,500 troops who were in the parade pass the saluting base where the General Officer Commanding Aldershot District and the Mayor of Aldershot take the salute. A high proportion of those taking part in the parade would have been National Servicemen.

Royal Army Service Corps barrack blocks, Oudenarde Barracks, Aldershot, 1949. When National Service was ended in 1960, rows of barrack blocks like this one were entirely demolished. Numbers of soldiers in Aldershot were to diminish significantly, and those who were part of the new military Aldershot would be quartered in four man rooms – the culture of barrack life would change significantly.

Eight
Leisure and Welfare

Soldiers outside Farnham United Breweries tent, Aldershot Manoeuvres, 1893. During manoeuvres, government contractors would frequently accompany troops. These would range from hay and forage suppliers, 'fizzer wallahs' who would sell aerated mineral water or breweries as shown here, keen to supply the needs of the soldiers.

Coffee Bar, Oxfordshire and Buckinghamshire Light Infantry, *c.* 1910. 'Respectable diversions' were an important aim for the Victorian and Edwardian military command. Coffee bars like this were part of the strategy developed by the War Office to discourage their soldiers from the drink and vice which could be found in most Garrison towns. Reading rooms, regimental institutes and coffee bars provided a venue outside of the barrack room, where soldiers could relax in their off duty hours. The coffee bars or canteens also provided food stuffs which could be purchased privately by the soldier to supplement his government food ration.

Reading Room, *c.* 1904. By the late nineteenth century, instruction in reading and writing was provided to soldiers who were illiterate. Differing grades of certificates were awarded as they progressed. Reading was not only a requirement now for everyone in an increasingly sophisticated Army, to enable them to perform their tasks, but was also encouraged as a diversion from 'lower forms of entertainment'. To this end reading rooms were provided for all, whereas initially they were the preserve of officers.

Regimental Games, Aldershot, 1904. Competitions in the Army were – and still are – a very important part of routine. Many competitions were formal sporting contests. Others like this, were regimental games, often using improvised equipment and rules. These images by local photographers Gale and Polden, record games whose rules are unknown to the author, and have probably long since passed into history.

Army Schools

THIS IS TO CERTIFY

that

Florence Robinson

was examined at *Aldershot* *by* *Elder Girls' School* ~~INSPECTOR OF ARMY SCHOOLS~~

on *10th to 12th May 1911.*

and passed in the following subjects

SUBJECTS	STANDARDS
Reading	4
Writing	4
Arithmetic	4
Needlework	5

R. Curtis COL.

COMMANDING R.E. TROOPS BOYS. Commanding Regt.

Certificate for Army Schooling, Royal Engineers School, Stanhope Lines, 1911. Not only was better provision for soldier's families being made in the form of married quartering, but also in the education of their children. These certificates were from one of a number of Army schools in Aldershot, which provided education until the age of twelve.

North Camp Brigade School, *c.* 1905. Although the original camp at Aldershot had made provision for schools through the allocations of huts, it wasn't until the 1890s that purpose built schools first appeared. This school still stands today, in use for very young families of military personnel.

Children's party group, Aldershot Married Quarters, *c.* 1920.

Military canteen, Bramshot, *c.* 1915. During the First World War, large areas surrounding Aldershot were brought into use as temporary barracks and training areas. Some of these camps offered few amenities. At Bramshot, where large numbers of Canadians were based, at least the spartan comforts of this canteen were available.

Navy Army and Air Force Institute Club, Aldershot, *c.* 1950. Born out of servicemen's needs in the First World War, the NAAFI was formed in 1921. Amongst the services it provided, a number of clubs were opened, including this one in Aldershot in 1948, known as the Roundabout Club. Changing patterns of leisure amongst servicemen led to eventual closure of this club, the building being demolished in 1987.

Royal Army Medical Corps at rest on Manoeuvres, 1905. These men are using their spare time to play cards, or repair clothing.

Soldiers catching up on the news from Cassidy's Newsagents, North Camp, Farnborough, 1912. The wagon seen was paid for by the *Daily Telegraph*, enabling the newspaper to be delivered to soldiers. The cart was driven to the manoeuvre area and the papers collected from the nearest railway station. It was the only cart financed in this way by the *Daily Telegraph*.

A CORNER OF THE BREAD STORE
AT THE ARMY SERVICE CORPS BAKERY, ALDERSHOT.

Bread at Aldershot Supply Depot, *c.* 1910. For many years the standard daily ration in the Army was 1lb of bread per day and $\frac{3}{4}$lb of meat. This was only added to by the purchase of goods through a regimental canteen account. In the 1880s, the standard Army loaf weighed 4lb, and was divided into quarters for each man. An enquiry found that large quantities of the bread were not being eaten by soldiers. This was because the cheapest flour was being used, along with brewers, rather than a patent yeast. As a result the bread was very unappetizing and frequently discarded by soldiers. In a series of experiments at Aldershot, the yeast was improved and better quality flour was used. Finally it was ordered that the loaves be baked in 2lb size only. The results were impressive and bread wastage fell dramatically.

Bread baking at Supply Depot, Aldershot, 1908. Army bakers at Aldershot could produce bread in two ways. The first was through a large set of ovens – shown here – for production to meet the needs of troops in barracks. Whilst on manoeuvres however, field bakeries were established. These used a system of iron arches which formed ovens and were fed with heat through a system of fires in trenches. The lower image shows this in operation at an exercise near Thorn Hill.

Butchery at the Supply Depot, Aldershot, 1908. In addition to bread, meat was the other main component of the Victorian and Edwardian soldier's diet, until the First World War. The supply depot at Aldershot met both of these needs. For meat supply, the depot had a slaughtering facility able to meet the demands of the whole camp every day – at that time some 15,000 or more troops.

Military swimming baths, Aldershot, *c*. 1905. New gymnasium facilities were added to the military camp in the 1890s. These were supplemented in 1904, with the opening of the military swimming baths nearby, which are shown here. These baths continued in use until the 1980s when they were closed. The building remains standing but disused.

Parlour, Smith-Dorrien Soldiers Home, *c*. 1910. This was opened as a Methodist Home in 1908. It took its name from the General Officer Commanding in Aldershot at the time, Sir Horace Smith-Dorrien. The building itself still stands, though the interior is much changed, as it is now used as offices.

SUNDAYS AT 7

SMITH-DORRIEN
SOLDIERS' HOME
Queen's Avenue, Aldershot

FORCES PROGRAMME

MUSICAL, VOCAL
and ORCHESTRAL

COMMUNITY SINGING
TOPICAL TALKS

EVERY SUNDAY AT 7.0 p.m.

All Ranks Cordially Invited

JOHN DREW
(PRINTERS) LTD.
ALDERSHOT
33199

Poster, Smith-Dorrien Soldier's Home, *c.* 1930. Homes such as the Smith-Dorrien were designed to keep the soldiers away from the temptations of drink and vice which existed in Aldershot. Both of these were a continual cause of disruption and disease in garrisons all over the empire. The entertainment was supposed to improve the soldiers' moral welfare and encourage self improvement, as this programme demonstrates.

A drummer of a Highland Regiment dancing, 1904. Aldershot was the largest British Army Garrison anywhere in the world. It saw troops from all over England, Ireland, Scotland and Wales, many of whom brought their own forms of entertainment with them.

Canteen tent, Aldershot Tattoo, c. 1935. Here, participants in the tattoo – soldiers from the Coldstream Guards and a Highland Regiment, take a break and share a drink. As well as the long build up and rehearsals prior to the show, the tattoo itself went on for a week, with two performances every evening,

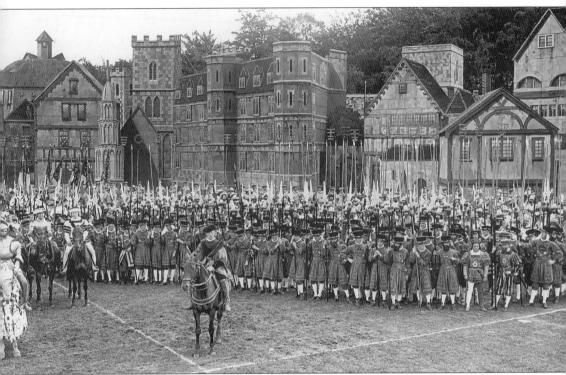

Historical Tableau, Aldershot Tattoo, 1939. Each of Aldershot's Tattoos between 1922 and 1939 had a different historical theme. To recreate scenes from various periods of history, elaborate lengths were gone to, to create huge sets as well as the costumes for the participants. There were complaints from officers at the time that the tattoo involved much time and effort, which would have been better expended on training for the troops, and other resources for additional activities.

Tattoo Evening Performance, c. 1935. Tattoo performances were generally held in the dark, and the second performances often did not finish until after midnight. Search lighting gave the tattoo its unique atmosphere. This was augmented by large numbers of torch bearers who would come on during the finale, forming illuminated patterns in the arena.

Come to The Greatest of all Shows

THE ALDERSHOT SHOW

• AT RUSHMOOR ARENA •
THURSDAY, FRIDAY & SATURDAY
JUNE 30TH & JULY 1ST & 2ND 1938

(Open 9.0 a.m. to 6.30 p.m.)

**HORSE AND HOUND SHOW :: MASSED BANDS
MUSICAL JUMPING RIDE—FULL DRESS
NOVEL TRICK RIDE—FANCY DRESS
MOTOR CYCLE TRICK RIDE
EMPIRE AND TRAVEL EXHIBITIONS**

ADMISSION DAILY (including Tax) 6/-, 2/6, 1/-.   CHILDREN 2/6, 1/2, 6d.

Car Parks, Numbered and Reserved, 5/-   Unreserved, 1/- or 2/6   Motor Bicycle, 1/-   Bicycle, 6d.
LUNCHEONS, REFRESHMENTS, TEAS, IN ALL ENCLOSURES
THE SOUTHERN RAILWAY will issue CHEAP TICKETS each day from Waterloo, and many Stations over a wide radius to Aldershot and Farnborough.
See Company's Bills.
ASK YOUR NEAREST MOTOR COACH OWNER FOR PARTICULARS OF CHEAP ROAD EXCURSIONS.

The Show of the Year

Advertisement for the Aldershot Show, 1938. The Show and Tattoo were two key parts of Aldershot's events calender. Both required considerable input by the Army, but in return gave Aldershot a high profile with the general public who came to the shows – the tattoo alone drew over 450,000 people in a week during the 1930s.

The Bob Potter band playing at the gymnasium, Deepcut, on the night before D-Day in June 1944 to an audience of Canadians who were based nearby. The objects in front of the stage are drill shells used for practise.

Navy Army and Air Force Institute supermarket, Talavera Park, c. 1965. Alongside the new married quarters of the 1960s military town, existed other facilities for the families of soldiers. These included a school and this unusual design of supermarket, arguably one of the most architecturally attractive buildings of its era in the area. Unfortunately, problems with its construction technique meant that this building was demolished in 1989 with the rest of the estate.

Nine
Technology

Balloon operated by Royal Engineers, Military Tournament Aldershot, c. 1900. The Royal Engineers Balloon Establishment had moved to Aldershot in the early 1890s. Balloons had been usefully employed by the British Army in South Africa in 1900 for spotting and observation purposes. They were eventually replaced by military airships and powered aircraft from 1908.

Maxim Gun Section, Aldershot, 1909. These maxim guns were manned by a visiting Territorial Force unit. By this time, the Vickers gun was under development, which would serve the British Army during the First World War. Mounting machine guns on wheeled carriages like these was stopped soon after this image was taken.

Royal Engineer Searchlight Section, c. 1904. Searchlights were used by the Royal Artillery from the 1890s, primarily for target illumination for coast artillery batteries. It wasn't until the 1920s that they were used against aircraft.

Army Signalling School, Thornhill, Aldershot, 1893. Aldershot's training role extended to all aspects of the Army. Before the formation of the Royal Corps of Signals in 1920, signalling was the responsibility of the Royal Engineers. Each regiment had to have its own trained signallers, competent in a number of different forms of message sending. This could be achieved in a number of different ways – the flags are obvious on many of the men here, but mirror signalling by Heliograph (shown on the right) or by lamp (on the left) were important methods as well.

Queens Edinburgh Rifle Volunteers at signalling practise, Aldershot, c. 1900. When assembled for signalling classes, men would form lines allowing sufficient space for each flag to be waved. Messages were sent using morse, shown as either a short or long stroke of the flag. A good signaller could show eight words per minute.

Maxim Machine Gun, Motor Volunteer Corps, mounted on a car during manoeuvres, Aldershot, c. 1910. The Victorian and Edwardian Army saw many experiments with new types of equipment, or with different methods of employing existing technology. Often these were done by Territorial units, as shown here. An absence of government-led research in many areas meant individuals had far more incentive to come up with new ideas to give them an advantage over a potential enemy.

Royal Engineers Wireless Station, Queens Avenue, Aldershot, c. 1915. Military wireless was still in it's infancy when this image was taken. In the trenches of France, most communication relied on telephone systems, or despatches via runner or pigeon.

Military Cyclists, *c*. 1914. Although the use of the bicycle had not proved very popular in the regular Army, the Territorials adopted them in some numbers. They were deemed to be particularly suitable for signalling parties, who could make could use of the extra mobility when placed on reconnaissance duties.

Transport Section, 7th (Service) Battalion East Surrey Regiment, Aldershot, 1915. Most of the British Army's transport in the First World War was still horse-drawn. However, transport in the war was not confined to wagons. A whole host of specialist vehicles were horse-drawn. These included forges, cable laying wagons, ambulances and field cookers, shown here.

Trooper, 7th Hussars, c. 1930. The first of the old horsed cavalry regiments to be mechanized did so in Aldershot in 1927. For those regiments still horsed, this was a typical turnout. By then the adoption of khaki had replaced the pre-1914 scarlet and blue uniforms. Also shown here is the modern bolt action rifle in addition to the sword which was still carried. These changes however were not to prevent the horse's final exit from the battlefield.

Military vehicles assembled in Rushmoor Arena at Aldershot, 1926. During the First World War there was considerable progress towards mechanization, particularly in logistics units. The growth of mechanization is well illustrated with these vehicles held in readiness as aid to the civil power during the General strike.

'D' Battery, Royal Horse Artillery, Aldershot, 1937. By this time, most of the Army was mechanized. Despite their name, the Royal Horse Artillery were no exception to the process of mechanization. Here, early tracked vehicles not only pull the guns, but also provided transport for the gun detachments. The cars in front are also fitted for wireless which was universal by the 1930s.

Inspection of Royal Artillery at Waterloo Barracks, Aldershot, 1932. This fascinating image of the Royal Artillery on parade clearly shows part of the slow transition being made towards mechanization in the inter-war years. In the fore ground are 4.5 inch Howitzers with their

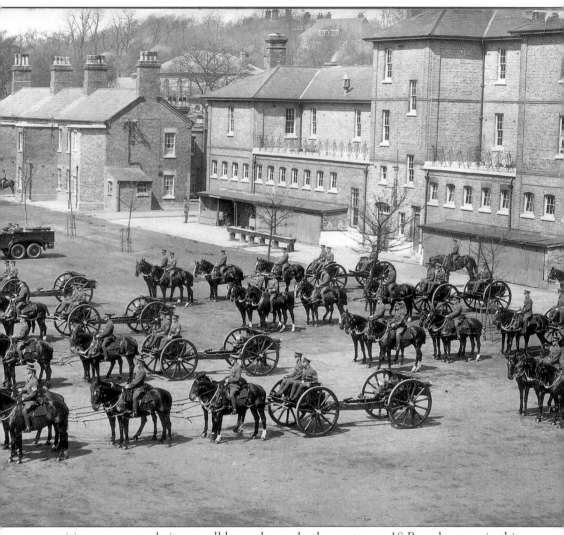

ammunition wagons to their rear, all horse drawn. In the centre are 18 Pounder guns, in this case however drawn by tracked vehicles. Similarly the officers in front of the mechanized guns are in cars, rather than on chargers.

Territorial Army unit with Search light, Bourley Road, near Aldershot, 1936. This photograph was taken during the summer camp of the First Surrey Rifles, when a Territorial Army unit had been converted to operate this new type of equipment. At this time the unit was quartered in camp at Mytchett. Despite retrenchment in defence spending during the 1930s, there was a concerted effort to prepare Britain for anti-aircraft warfare. This included not only the formation of Search Light Units, but also the development of the anti-aircraft guns with which they would operate.

Light Tanks of the Fife and Forfar Yeomanry, Long Valley, Aldershot, 1940. Aldershot's Cavalry Brigade had passed into history by the time these tanks were passing over the ground which had witnessed the great Royal Reviews of Horse and Foot. Virtually all of Britain's cavalry regiments had been mechanized. New training areas around Salisbury Plain were giving the Army much needed training areas, to supercede those at Aldershot which were too small for large scale mechanized manoeuvres.

Ten
Departures

Men returning from South Africa, Aldershot railway station, May 1901. Aldershot sent a number of volunteers to fight in South Africa, mostly drawn from the town's volunteer company of the Hampshire Regiment. The returning volunteers can be distinguished by their slouch hats.

Trooper of the 12th Lancers, Long Valley, Aldershot, 1899. On the outbreak of the South African (or Boer) War in October 1899, the whole of Aldershot's cavalry brigade was immediately equipped and mobilized for the campaign. This image taken just prior to their departure shows the standard equipment of every man and horse. The campaign dragged on for nearly three years and many important lessons were hard learnt by the British, not least of which was the importance of proper veterinary care for its horses which died in huge numbers.

Medal parade, Aldershot, 1901. Men here receive their South African War medals from Maj.-Gen. Robert Baden-Powell. Baden-Powell had achieved fame during the war for holding out against Boer Forces in the Siege of Mafeking. The presentation here is taking place at one of Aldershot's cavalry barracks.

Unveiling of the Royal Army Medical Corps South African War Memorial, 1905. Aldershot had provided the bulk of the Army's initial mobilization for the South African War. This memorial to men of the RAMC who gave their lives, was built on Gun Hill where it still stands today.

Departures of troops for the First World War, Aldershot, 1914. The image above shows one of the regular regiments quartered in Aldershot in 1914 – the Cameronians (Scottish Rifles). They are marching down the Farnborough Road, where today the busy Wellington roundabout is located. Below, a 'New Army' regiment in Wellington Lines. They can be distinguished by the obsolete pattern rifles they carry.

SERGEANTS MESS 7TH BTN: E. SURREY REGT: ALDERSHOT. 1915

Sergeants' Mess, 7th (Service) Battalion East Surrey Regiment, Aldershot, 1915. Aldershot became a huge transit camp during the First World War, mobilizing complete divisions, and providing drafts to the British Army in France and other parts of the world. This battalion was part of the 12th (Eastern) Division, a 'Kitchener' division which was heavily employed on the Western Front. It left Aldershot in late May 1915 and by the time the war had ended this division alone had suffered 41,000 casualties.

Also shown is Sgt B.C. Samuda, a member of the sergeants mess of the battalion, who survived the war.

Regiment.	Names of Officers and numbers ordered.	Names of Officers and numbers proceeded.	Date of departure
11th Hussars	Four Signallers		
15th Hussars	Four Signallers	As ordered.	9-4-18.
19th Hussars	Four Signallers.		

War Office telegram No. 553 A.G.5 dated 5-4-18.
H.Q.,

Aldershot,
...9th April....1918.

Colonel,
Commanding 3rd Reserve Regiment of Hussars

Report of Departure of Drafts, 3rd Reserve Regiment of Hussars, 9 April 1918. Reserve cavalry regiments based in Aldershot during the First World War provided regular reinforcements to the British Army on France and Belgium. Here, twelve signallers are ordered for service.

The Citizens of Aldershot

request the Honour of the Presence of

M. A. Tanner.

At Maida Drill Hall, Queen's Avenue, on Saturday,
May 24th (Empire Day), 1919

on the occasion of

Aldershot's Welcome Home to Townsmen

who have served in the Armed Forces of the

Crown during the Great War, 1914-1918

PUBLIC WELCOME,
MUNICIPAL GARDENS, 4 P.M.

RECEPTION AT
MAIDA DRILL HALL, 5 P.M.

This Invitation Card must be Presented at the doors

Invitation to welcome home, Maida Gymnasium, 1919. At the end of the First World War, Aldershot Urban District Council organized a welcome home for all of its residents who had served in the war.

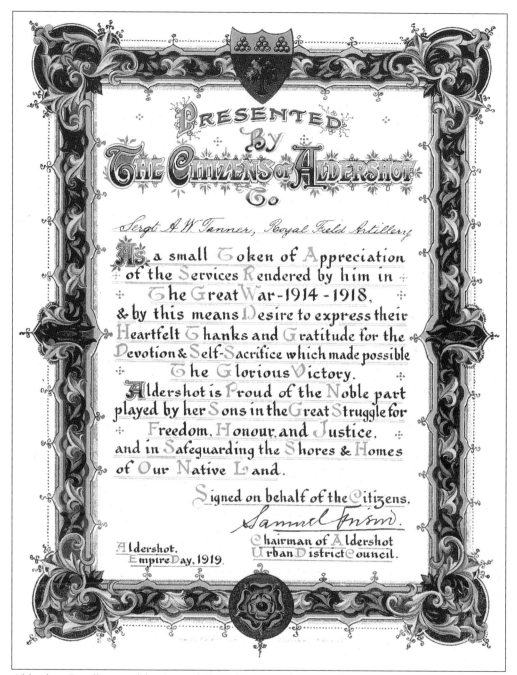

PRESENTED BY THE CITIZENS OF ALDERSHOT TO

Sergt. A.W. Tanner, Royal Field Artillery

As a small Token of Appreciation of the Services Rendered by him in The Great War - 1914 - 1918, & by this means Desire to express their Heartfelt Thanks and Gratitude for the Devotion & Self-Sacrifice which made possible The Glorious Victory. Aldershot is Proud of the Noble part played by her Sons in the Great Struggle for Freedom, Honour, and Justice, and in Safeguarding the Shores & Homes of Our Native Land.

Signed on behalf of the Citizens.

Samuel Friend.

Chairman of Aldershot Urban District Council.

Aldershot.
Empire Day, 1919.

Aldershot Scroll, signed by Samuel Friend, 1919. These scrolls were presented by Aldershot Urban District Council to every town's person who had served in the war. This one was presented to Arthur William Tanner, who had joined the Royal Artillery Mounted Band in 1913. During the war he found himself posted to a Royal Field Artillery Battery as a clerk and served for the duration of the war on the Western Front.

Departure of Royal Artillery Mounted Rifles for Ireland, 1921. In the years immediately following the First World War, civil unrest in Ireland meant that many of the troops who would otherwise have been in garrison at Aldershot were deployed to Ireland, in support of

the already large garrison stationed there. The men are shown in front of the Royal Artillery
Barracks in Wellington Lines.

Aldershot Branch, Toc H, 1925. In Belgium during the First World War, a soldiers club was founded in Poperinghe. It was known as Talbot House, or Toc H for short. The club provided off-duty soldiers with a quiet place for rest and relaxation. Following the war many ex-soldiers wanted to recreate the atmosphere of Toc H, so branches were set up all over the country from 1920.

Unveiling of a war memorial to the 8th Division, Aldershot, 1921. The 8th Division was formed at Aldershot on the outbreak of the First World War. This memorial was erected near to the Aldershot Command Headquarters, where it remains a familiar landmark to this day.

Display of brick making by the Army Vocational Training Establishment, Aldershot Horse Show, 1933. Following the end of the First World War the Army took re-training of soldiers for life outside of the Army more seriously. The Army Vocational Training Centre in Aldershot provided soldiers with the opportunity to learn mainly manual skills. These included plumbing, lead work, plastering, concrete work, or brick work as shown in this exhibition tent. The centre built some houses in Galwey Road in Aldershot, some of which still stand today. Responsibility for retraining passed to the Ministry of Labour in 1938, and the centre was closed after only fourteen years in existence.

Sergeant James Connell, 4th Hussars, 1933. James Connell joined the 6th Dragoon Guards in 1909. After a long career in the Army, which included the award of the Military Medal during the First World War, his career brought him to Willems Barracks in Aldershot. It was here that he served the last part of his twenty-seven years service. As a highly competent cavalry man, he was well known for his trick riding skills. The second picture demonstrates his skills: here he had trained his horse to sit down in a very unconventional manner!

Aldershot Branch, Royal British Legion, *c.* 1955. The Aldershot Branch made Maj.-Gen. W. Dimoline, General Officer Commanding at Aldershot, an honorary member. He is seen here addressing the meeting. On his right is Lt-Col. H.N. Cole TD, a former commanding officer of an Aldershot Territorial Army unit, who was president of the branch at the time.

South African War Veterans Association, Evensong Service, Royal Garrison church, Aldershot, 1966. For many ex-servicemen who have connections with the area, Aldershot has been a place for reunion and pilgrimage over the years. This was the last evensong service held for veterans of the South African War (1899-1902). The Royal Garrison church also hosted the annual service of the Old Contemptibles, the survivors of Britain's regular Army which travelled to France in 1914. These reunions stopped in 1974.

The Parachute Regiment marching to Aldershot railway station *en route* to Suez, 1956. Until the 1960s, most troop movements were undertaken by sea. It was customary for troops leaving Aldershot to undertake the first stage of their journey via the railway which would normally take them to Southampton. In the back ground is the South Western Hotel which was partially demolished in the late 1950s.

House Clearing Exercise, Talavera Barracks, *c.* 1960. This soldier uses part of Aldershot's redundant Victorian barracks prior to their demolition. Since 1969, operations in Northern Ireland have meant that it has been necessary for many soldiers to become familiar with functioning in urban environments.

Theatre productions like this one were a popular means of entertainment for soldiers before the arrival of cinema. They also kept soldiers occupied and away from the temptations of vice which existed in Aldershot at the time.

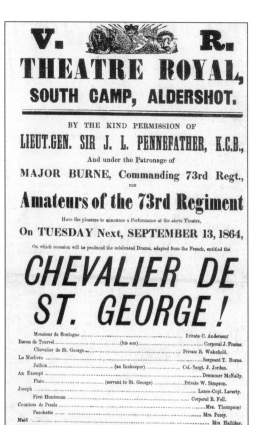

of the 73rd Regiment.

THE
Amateurs of the 73rd REGIMENT
Will make their first appearance at the above Theatre,

On TUESDAY NEXT, OCTOBER 13th, 1863,

In Douglas Jerrold's celebrated Drama of

THE RENT DAY.

Squire Grantley	(of Grantley Hall)	Corporal Probert.
Old Crumbs	(his steward)	Private C. Anderson.
Martin Heywood	(a farmer)	Corporal Bettington.
Toby Heywood	(his brother)	Corporal Wakefield.
Bulfrog	(auctioneer, appraiser, and estate agent)	Private H. Hazard.
Silver Jack and Hyssop	(knights of the road)	Sergt. Bishop & Corp. Frames.
Beanstalk		Corporal Smith.
Stephen		Private M'Nally.
Farmers		Private Williams and Corporal Jones.
Bourley		Corporal Walsh.
Sailor		Private Jones.
Rachel Heywood		Mrs. H. Percy.
Polly Briggs		Mrs. J. Stoner.

Tenants, Villagers, &c.

TO BE FOLLOWED BY

A COMIC SONG ...... Private H. Hazard.

The performance to conclude with Maddison Morton's Laughable Farce of

A Thumping Legacy,
OR
A TALE OF CORSICA.

Filippo Geronimo		Corporal Bettington.
Jerry Ominum	(of St. Mary-Axe, London)	Sergeant Bishop.
Leoni		Private Williams.
(a young Corsican)		Corporal Wakefield.
Brigadier of Carabineers		Private C. Anderson.
Carabineers		Privates Smith & Walsh.
Rosetta	(daughter of Filippo)	Mrs. H. Percy.

By the kind permission of Lieut.-Col. Jones the BAND of the 73rd Regiment will attend and perform several Popular Selections.

Reserved Seats, 2s. ; Pit, 1s. ; Gallery, 6d.

Doors open at Eight p.m. Performances to commence at Half-past Eight.

Tickets to be obtained from the Sergeant-Majors and Colour-Sergeants of Companies, and at the Doors of the Theatre on the night of the performance.

VIVAT REGINA.

W. SHELDRAKE, Army Printer, Aldershot.

A poster for a theatrical production by the 73rd Regiment, printed by William Sheldrake, 1863.

A Comic Song . . . . . . Private J. CROSBIE.

AFTER WHICH,

To conclude with the laughable Farce of

MORE BLUNDERS THAN ONE !

Harry Melbourne		Drummer McNally.
Old Melbourne		Private C. Anderson.
Trap	(a Bailiff)	Col.-Sergt. Mulcahey.
Larry Hooligan	(a Bad Boy)	Col.-Sergt. Jordan.
Louisa		Mrs. Percy.
Susan	(her Maid)	Mrs. Thompson.
Jenny		Mrs. Halliday.

Doors open at 8.30, Performance to commence at 9 o'clock, p.m.

By the kind Permission of Major Burne, the Band of the Regiment will be in attendance.

PRICES OF ADMISSION:

Gallery	- - - - - - - - - - -	0s. 6d.
Pit	- - - - - - - - - - -	1s. 0d.
Stalls	- - - - - - - - - - -	2s. 0d.

Tickets to be obtained from the Sergeant-Major, Color-Sergeants of Companies, and at the Doors on the Night of the Performance.

VIVAT REGINA !

W. SHELDRAKE, Army and Machine Printer, High-street, Aldershot.

Another Victorian theatre bill.

To all Military & Police Authorities.

No. _____

Permit the Driver of

Fill in for one vehicle only, two must be struck out.

Lorry No. .... Foden No. .... Car No. ....

belonging to the Aldershot and District Traction Coy., Limited, to travel within your area with Moderate Lights, on urgent Military Service.

(By Order.)

S. H. LYNN, Colonel,

A.D. of S. & T. Aldershot Command.

Head Quarters,
Aldershot,
29th January, 1915.

NOTICE TO DRIVERS.

All drivers must be careful to see they have the permit for the particular vehicle they are driving, and in all cases where the driver changes vehicles, he is to hand in the permit and obtain the correct one before taking out the new vehicle.

military driving permit, 1915.